the Angel in COLLECT

To
Mrs Toop
My Book of Heavenly Ways
Love Jacob Davenport
x

About the Artist

Deb Haas Abell lives with her husband and two children in a cosy home with a picket fence, nestled in a small town in Southern Indiana. She hopes this book will put you in touch with heavenly help and healing . . . and the angel in you!

About the Author

Molly Wigand lives in suburban Kansas City with her husband and three angelic sons. She's grateful to be able to share her thoughts and feelings with you.

Heavenly Ways to Grow Closer as a Family

Created and Illustrated by Deb Haas Abell

Written by Molly Wigand

Text © 1998 by Molly Wigand
Art © 1998 by Deb Haas Abell
Published by Eagle Publishing
PO Box 530, Guildford,
Surrey GU2 5FH

All rights reserved.
No part of this book may be used or reproduced in any manner
without written permission of the publisher, except in the case
of brief quotations embodied in critical articles and reviews.

ISBN 0-86347-3288

Printed in Malta

The Angel in Your Family

The joys of home and family are among our most precious blessings. Yet our hectic, stressful lifestyles sometimes threaten family harmony and together times. Thankfully, every family has a guiding angel, helping us to share God's unconditional love with one another.

The insights in this book are offered to help your family get in touch with your special angel. Feel free to jot your thoughts and feelings on the write-on activity pages, or to keep your reflections privately in your heart.

May this book help you share your God-given angel's message of joyful acceptance: you are welcome and safe in this family. God's love and compassion are with you, helping you grow closer to one another.

All the Comforts of Home

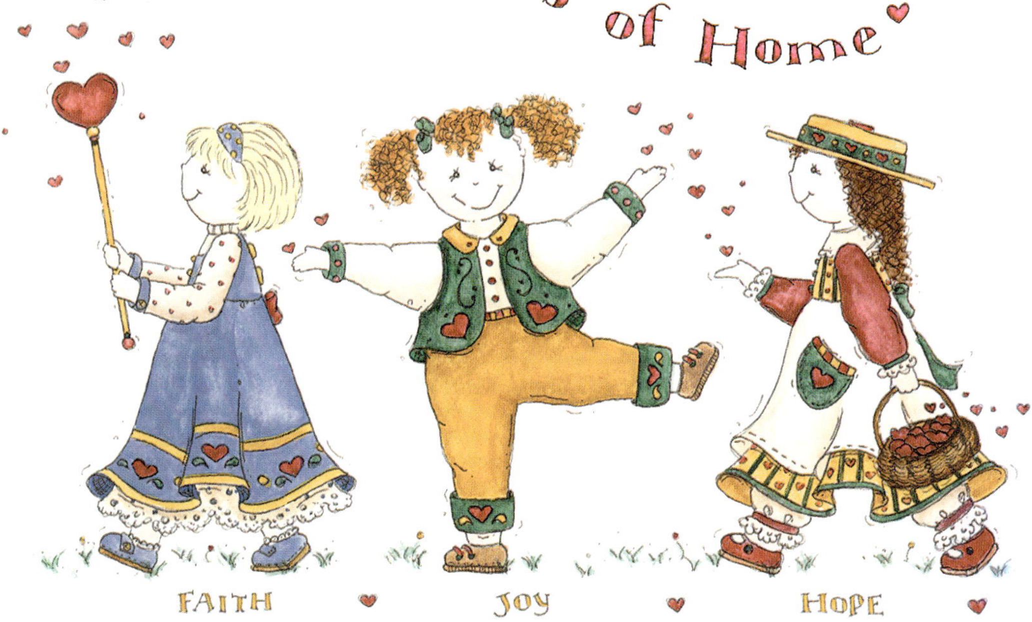

Raising a happy family is one of life's most important endeavours. The gifts we receive from family time enrich our lives and make us better human beings. By renewing our commitment to being a good family member, we honour our family as the blessing it truly is.

HARMONY ♥ CHARITY ♥ GRACE ♥ GOODNESS

Home Is Where the Heart Is

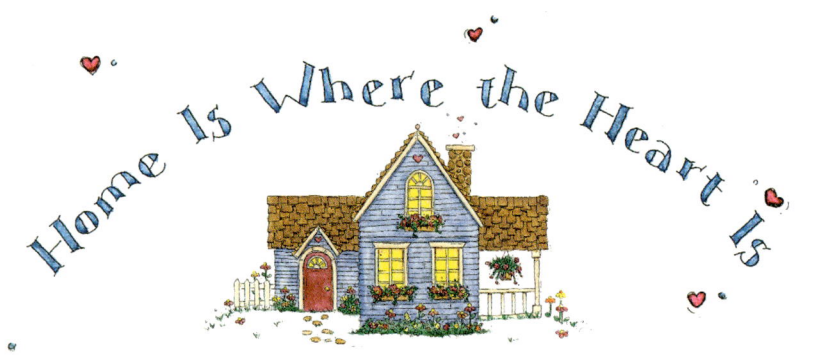

We tend to take for granted the people who support and encourage us every day.

When you wake up tomorrow morning, acknowledge the wonderful connection you have with your family members. Even if they snore or hog the telephone or throw clothes on the floor, their presence in your life is a blessing.

Ask your family's guardian angel to remind you gently of the value and worth of each human being . . . especially those at home!

Have You Told Them Lately?

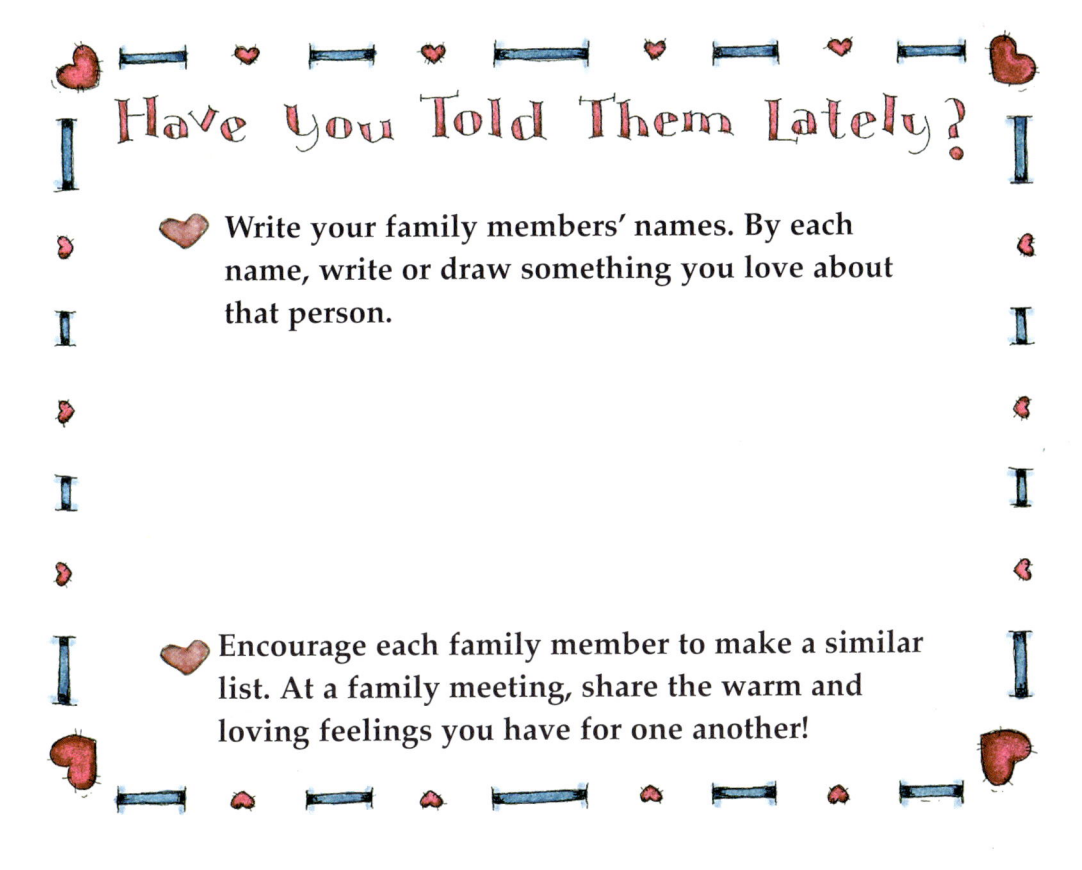

♥ Write your family members' names. By each name, write or draw something you love about that person.

♥ Encourage each family member to make a similar list. At a family meeting, share the warm and loving feelings you have for one another!

Try to Remember...

Joy

Families go through many stages filled with reasons for joy and thankfulness. The day of your marriage, your children's births, establishing new homes and making new friends are milestones that contribute to your rich family history.

These shared experiences give depth and meaning to your home life, and they provide a solid family foundation to withstand life's problems and conflicts.

Tell Me a Story

Grandparents' stories delight children and help us all understand our special place on the family tree. Encourage older relatives to share their stories. Encourage children to retell the stories or record them for posterity.

With your family angel's help, your children will appreciate the wisdom grandparents and other older family members possess.

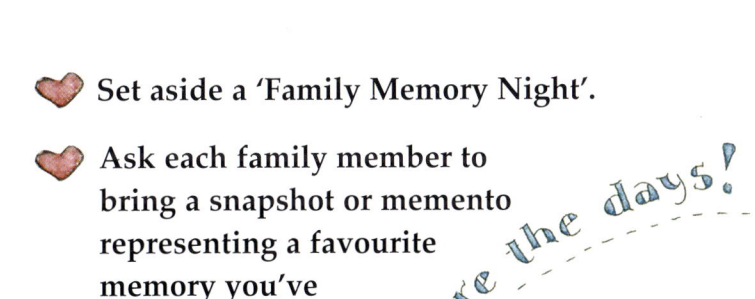

- Set aside a 'Family Memory Night'.
- Ask each family member to bring a snapshot or memento representing a favourite memory you've shared.
- Write everyone's favourite family memory right here:

Those were the days!

God's Kids

The Bible refers to human beings as the children of God. We are all part of God's loving family and we are encouraged to follow God's example in our earthly families and homes.

Let your family angel show you the goodness and love within your own family, and help you think about the ties you share with the whole human family.

Love One Another...
No Matter What!

It's easy to fall into a pattern of complaining to others about the people we love – griping about tiring toddlers, trying teenagers or sloppy spouses.

Yet these complaints can encourage negative, critical thoughts to take hold, and we may eventually lose track of our purpose as family members. It's when children and spouses are their least lovable that they need our love the most.

Ask your angel to help you find kind and loving words to use when you talk about the most important people in your life.

I ♥ My Family

♥ Write a positive thought about each member of your family.

♥ Promise you'll share these loving messages instead of petty complaints in your conversations this week.

Harmony

At Home in the Universe

Just as we are God's children, the universe God created is our home. By experiencing and appreciating our roles as guardians and caretakers of nature, we can better understand our responsibility to care for our own homes and families.

God accepts and cares for every part of creation, from the tiniest sparrow to the tallest redwood tree. With our angel's help, we can learn to accept the diversity and uniqueness of people both inside and outside our families.

Keep in Touch... With Nature!

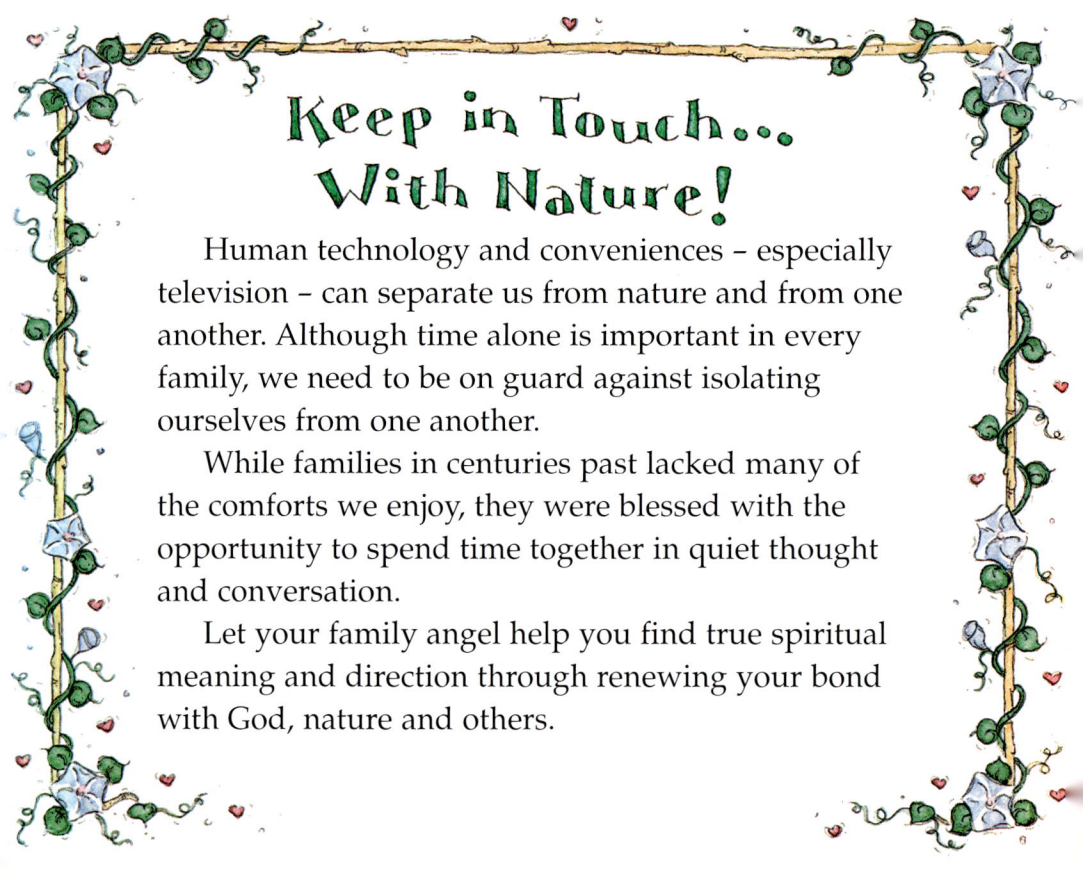

Human technology and conveniences – especially television – can separate us from nature and from one another. Although time alone is important in every family, we need to be on guard against isolating ourselves from one another.

While families in centuries past lacked many of the comforts we enjoy, they were blessed with the opportunity to spend time together in quiet thought and conversation.

Let your family angel help you find true spiritual meaning and direction through renewing your bond with God, nature and others.

Lights Out!

- ♥ Choose a night in the near future to be 'Pioneer Night'. Pretend the electricity to your home is cut off, your cars are in the garage, and your telephone lines are down.

- ♥ Cook dinner in the fireplace (or eat 'pioneer food' that doesn't need cooking). Each family member is responsible for leading one 'low-tech' activity – a board game, jigsaw puzzle, or charades for example.

- ♥ Did your family make it through the night without modern conveniences? What insights did you gain?

Are We Having Fun Yet?

Happy Times

Peaceful Moments

Too often, we develop a 'firefighter' attitude towards our families: we don't notice what's going on unless there's a 'fire' to put out!

Your family angel can help you acknowledge and appreciate the joyful and harmonious times you share. By becoming mindful of your family's happy and peaceful moments, you will gain confidence and can keep the inevitable challenging situations in perspective.

Something's Got to Give!

Being a giving family member requires sorting through many demands on our time and energy: career, friends, volunteer commitments. It's important to remember that overcommitment to outside obligations can be detrimental to a family.

Workplaces and schools stress the importance of prioritising your tasks. Ask your family's angel for help in making time to enjoy one another.

Time Management~ Angel Style

- Gather your family together. Compare your schedules for the coming week.

- Subtract one 'optional' activity from each family member's schedule.

- What will you do with your 'found time'? A fun family outing? Dinner and a film? Or simply a few moments of peace and quiet with the most important people in your life?

Way to go!

Charity

Charity Does Begin at Home

Within the haven of home, we find love that never ends, and care for special needs and hurts.

Sympathetic hugs, sincere thank-yous and praise for jobs well done are angelic acts of kindness, which renew the spirits and kindle the love in family members.

That's What Families Are For

When a spouse becomes withdrawn or a child's school work suffers, it may be a sign of a problem.

Your family's angel can help you cultivate an atmosphere of open communication, helping family members help each other through difficult times.

Listen and Learn

❤ To nurture family communication and get feelings and concerns out in the open, try this variation on the Native American 'talking stick' ritual.

❤ Have your family choose a twig to use in the ceremony.

❤ Beginning with the youngest person, allow each family member to hold the 'talking stick' while expressing thoughts and feelings about the family, the world or life in general. Only the person holding the stick may speak. Pass the stick around the table. Each person may respond to what's been said or express his or her own thoughts, feelings and concerns.

What insights did you gain?

Do Unto Others

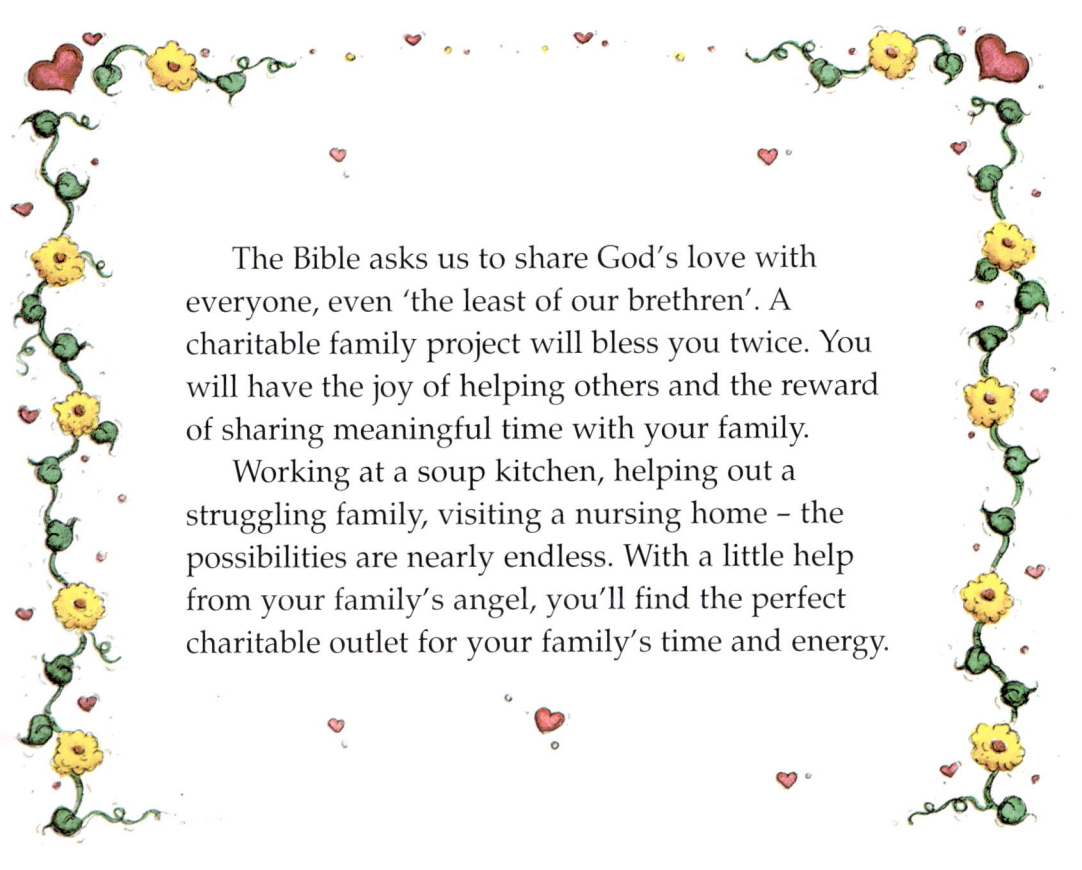

The Bible asks us to share God's love with everyone, even 'the least of our brethren'. A charitable family project will bless you twice. You will have the joy of helping others and the reward of sharing meaningful time with your family.

Working at a soup kitchen, helping out a struggling family, visiting a nursing home – the possibilities are nearly endless. With a little help from your family's angel, you'll find the perfect charitable outlet for your family's time and energy.

Home Away From Home

Reach out to those less fortunate friends whose families are far away or unavailable to offer love and support.

With your angel's help, you can be an 'adoptive family' for friends who desperately need the safe, secure feeling of 'home'.

There's Always Room for One More!

❤ Who are some people you know who could use the acceptance of a loving family?

❤ Invite these friends to a fun family gathering. Offer your family's friendship and support.

Hope

Safe at Home

Every day, newspapers and television remind us that the world can be a scary place to raise a family. International conflicts, government scandals, violent crime and drugs may seem to strike fearfully close to the people we love and the values we hold dear.

Your family's angel can help keep your home a place of hope and safety both for your family and for others whose lives you touch. When your family opens its heart to goodness and optimism, God will help you discover the beauty and good in the world around you.

Everyone Needs a Security Blanket

Even the most positive, optimistic family encounters worry and anxiety from time to time. During a parent's illness, children may fear that parent's death. During arguments, children may fear divorce. Parents, too, experience legitimate concerns about finances, health and child-raising.

Your family's angel can remind you that prayer works wonders. God's loving-kindness will ease your worries and bring peace to your family's hearts.

❤ Make a Worry Box. Have each family member write their worries on index cards and drop them in the box.

❤ At the end of each day, talk out the worries. Turn those that are out of your control over to God.

❤ As a family, brainstorm ways to ease each person's worries. Ask your family's angel to share God's wisdom and guidance with you.

I Love Ya, Tomorrow!

Help family members be patient and optimistic if problems don't disappear overnight. Trust God to transform family cares and worries, deepening faith and strengthening family ties.

Believe that the dark trials and turmoil of today will look brighter in the light of a new day. Look to your family's angel to reveal God's purpose and plan.

The Stuff Families Are Made Of

One of the brightest joys of family is sharing plans and dreams. In the safe, nurturing haven of home, each family member's potential can flourish. Individual and family visions beckon us towards a future filled with hope, optimism and joy.

Ask your angel to guide your family's hopes and dreams in a meaningful and wise direction.

'Un-Birthday' Wishes!

💗 With your family, bake an 'un-birthday cake'. Light one 'un-birthday' candle for each family member.

💗 Have each person make a special wish. Encourage children to wish for spiritual gifts rather than presents or toys. Record the wishes here.

💗 Have the youngest child blow out the candles.

Nurture an atmosphere of forgiveness and acceptance.

Grace

No Family's Perfect

It's human nature to reserve our most negative and unlovable behaviour for the people we're closest to. We inevitably experience impatience and aggravation with the people whose shortcomings we're exposed to every day.

Just as God forgives the family of humankind, healthy families nurture an atmosphere of forgiveness and acceptance. The angel in your family can foster openness and understanding, creating a home environment filled with heavenly grace.

Clearing the Air

Even in the most open family, resentment and anger can go unexpressed and unresolved. Family members may clam up or act out negative feelings in hurtful ways.

Holding a family meeting can air conflicts and get family communication back on track. These meetings might seem risky or frightening – family members may not want to 'rock the boat' by expressing 'negative' feelings. But openness and honesty will bring abundant rewards to your family as trust and intimacy grow.

Just Say, "I'm Sorry"

- ♥ Think back on a time when you were unkind or inconsiderate to a family member.
- ♥ Write a heartfelt apology. Share your apology with the person you hurt, and accept forgiveness.

♥ A Heartfelt Apology ♥

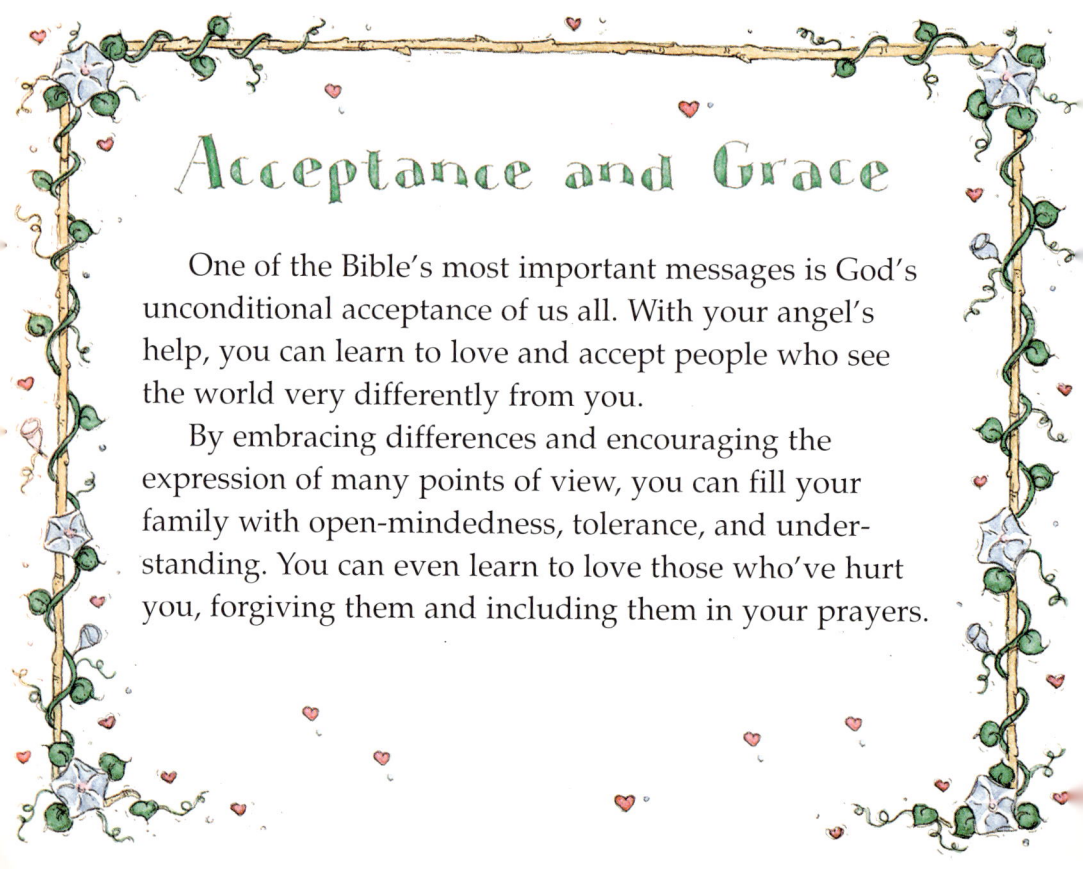

Acceptance and Grace

One of the Bible's most important messages is God's unconditional acceptance of us all. With your angel's help, you can learn to love and accept people who see the world very differently from you.

By embracing differences and encouraging the expression of many points of view, you can fill your family with open-mindedness, tolerance, and understanding. You can even learn to love those who've hurt you, forgiving them and including them in your prayers.

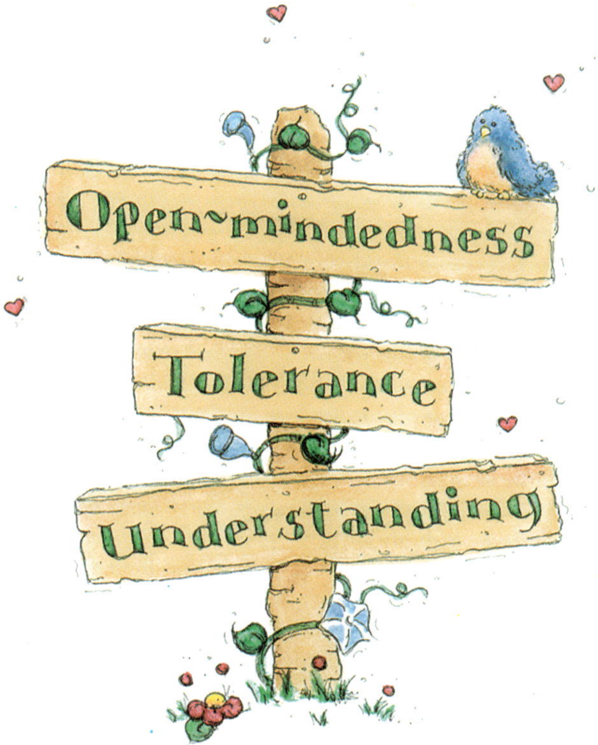
Open~mindedness
Tolerance
Understanding

A Garden of Gratitude

The stress of raising a family can overwhelm us at times. We may find our thoughts filled with resentment and self-pity over the many demands on our time and energy.

When this happens, your inner angel can remind you of the blessings God has given . . . most importantly, the gift of loving and being loved.

Acknowledging the bounty of our lives – food, clothing, shelter, companionship – replaces our frustrations with gratitude and joy.

One Big, Grateful Family!

❤️ Gather your family together to write a thank-you note to God.

❤️ Have each child and parent write one sentence expressing thanks for a blessing the family enjoys. Refer to the letter when stress and conflict weigh on your hearts and minds.

Let Go and Let God

Faith

Developing a loving, caring, accepting family is an important and serious responsibility. Our children's moral growth and development depends on the lessons and insights they learn at home.

Fortunately, none of us has to do it alone. God's strength and guidance are yours for the asking. With the help of the angel in your family, your home can become a reflection of God's plan for us all.

Heavenly Peace

By nurturing our family members as spiritual beings, we enrich their lives and strengthen their hearts. Whether you belong to a church congregation or practise your beliefs in another way, God wants to bless your family with the peace and meaning only faith can bring.

With your inner angel's help, you can find a place for worship, prayer and thanksgiving in your daily life, bringing you closer to God and to one another.

The Family That Prays Together

- Prayer is the spiritual link that connects families to the love of God. Praying together brings us closer to one another and to God's plan.

- Invite family members to join in a circle of prayer. With hands joined, take turns sharing family members' thanks, praise, sorrow and concerns. Encourage all to turn over every detail of their life to God's loving care.

Join in a circle of prayer.

Simply Divine!

God's plan for you includes loving and being loved by your family. The miracle of this plan is no less than the miracle of the universe.

Never forget that in the warmth and safety of your family, you are experiencing the love and affirming the goodness in God's creation. By staying mindful of the precious blessings of home and family, we become grateful and faithful family members, worthy of these priceless gifts.

Love and be loved

Every Family Is Blessed

Just as individual human beings reflect the diversity of God's universe, the families we live in display a rainbow of marvellous differences. Each family, with its unique heritage of traditions, values and beliefs, is part of God's plan to fill the earth with love, kindness, understanding – and variety!

Cherish and celebrate your own special family identity.

Comparing Notes

💗 Invite another family to dinner. Ask parents and children to share their ideas on growing closer as a family. In return, share your own suggestions for family enrichment.

💗 How can your friends' new ideas work for your family?

Family Matters!
Believe
Hope
Harmony
Faith
God bless
the
Angel in You
Charity
Joy
Grace

Although the blessings of home and family are among God's most precious gifts, all families experience times of worry, anger and sadness. The simple ideas in this book (or any book) may not always be enough to help you and your family through every difficult time.

Remember: God wants us to be happy. If stress and conflict begin to consume your family's reserves of peace and joy, seek the help of a wise friend, a doctor, a member of the clergy or a counsellor.

Keep Those Thoughts and Prayers Coming

'A happy family is but an earlier heaven', wrote one poet. With the help of God and your inner angel, your family will grow ever closer. By keeping your home and family at the heart of your thoughts and prayers, God's gifts of peace and happiness will bless your family every day.

❤ Create a special corner in your home dedicated to your family's angel. Display pictures of family members, special family mementos and this book.

A Little Bit of Heaven!

❤ Draw a picture of your angel watching over your family.

About the Heavenly Ways Books

Once upon an idea, in a little heartland village, an artist named Deb Haas Abell toiled away with her paintbrush and paints. Inspired by the many angels in her own life, she created six heart-sprinkling characters: Faith, Hope, Charity, Joy, Harmony and Grace. Their one mission in life was to spread the message that God gives each of us the ability to be an angel on earth . . . to touch lives, lighten hearts, and inspire souls.

Before long, they were introduced to writer Molly Wigand, who translated their wisdom into books like this one – about Heavenly Ways to cope, even in the midst of life's hardships and heartaches.

But this is not just another pretty fairy tale. For Faith, Hope, Charity, Joy, Harmon, and Grace are present every day inside each one of us! May these books help you to discover your own inner angel . . . and may God bless the angel in you!

Heavenly Ways Books

Heavenly Ways to Handle Stress
Heavenly Ways to Heal From Grief and Loss
Heavenly Ways to Grow Closer as a Family
Heavenly Ways to Find Your Own Serenity

Available at your favorite bookstore or directly from:
Eagle Publishing
PO Box 530, Guildford,
Surrey GU2 5FH